The Money Chi

V. John Alexandrov

Copyright 2005 – All Rights Reserved
V. John Alexandrov

ISBN 1-59975-267-0

www.themoneychi.com

Definitions

Money – a means of expressing oneself through the use of currency.

Economy – the sum total of our individual thoughts.

Chi – vital essence; the fundamental energy that sustains life; the sustaining energy of the Universe.

God – YOUR…Higher Power, Infinite Intelligence, Source Of All, Divine Essence…however YOU define God.

"Avail yourself of the force of the Universe,
And bring your instinctive ability into full play."
Wang Xiang Zhai

"The journey home to our natural greatness seems difficult at first, but then we realize we can observe every mystery and be present at every moment – this is the gateway to indescribable marvels."
V. John Alexandrov (paraphrasing Lao Tzu)

Introduction

The Universe is a live, pulsating, ever-expanding vital essence. The Universe is on a mission: to expand, to grow and to prosper. Every living, breathing energy force plays a unique and necessary role in this mission. Every day, in some way, each of us can experience this growth. Each of us can prosper in ways that may at first seem impossible. Thank goodness the Universe doesn't recognize impossibilities; the Universe only understands possibilities.

You are about to experience a quantum leap in your understanding of your individual (and collective) potential to tap into the power of the Universe and expand your life to the highest levels of happiness and joy. Simply put, the principles and exercises in this book will allow you to understand your abilities to create an individual (and collective) economy in which you are free to express yourself through the manifestation and use of money.

My immediate mission is to help you create a personal economic system that creates a reverence for all life. God (however YOU define God) needs a body and you are that body. As you expand your abilities to create and attract money through the proper application(s) of the principles in this book (and others you will find at our website – *www.themoneychi.com*), the value you will add to the world will literally change the world.

Imagine a world with no scarcity, no lack or deprivation, no fear or "needs." Imagine a world where money flows easily, effortlessly and continuously in ever-increasing amounts. Imagine a world where everything is within your reach spiritually, physically and mentally. Imagine a world of perfect grace, perfect abundance and perfect acceptance. Imagine there is an ***exact science*** to attracting everything and anything to which you are entitled. Imagine it is your heritage to experience complete joy in every way.

You just experienced the ***Truth...***

Chapter 1

Money Is Good!

What a powerful statement. Money is Good! You may ask, "What do you mean when you say money is good? I learned money is the root of all evil. I learned a camel would fit through the eye of a needle before a rich man could enter the kingdom of heaven. I learned money doesn't grow on trees." Well you learned a distorted, unfounded set of paradigms that has created and perpetuated fear, greed, lack and disempowerment for generations.

Money has been "a source of pain" throughout history. Religious orders have renounced it. Vows of "poverty" have been taken. Beliefs arose that poverty is a virtue. It all sounds so righteous.

The simple truth, however, is that money is innocent. Money is pure. Money doesn't care where it goes. The only thing that can distort the decency of money is our attitudes and paradigms towards it. Money is a resource, always at our beckon and call, just waiting to be summoned for our intended use.

You (yes YOU) have the ability to create a new blue print of prosperity consciousness. You are the architect and builder of your own reality. You can create a life of permanent financial independence; your own economy of limitless supply, and you can do so without limiting anyone else's power to do the same.

The Money Chi principles are absolute. They have been employed by money "geniuses" for thousands of years. The principles have been proven time and again. Now it's your turn to be a money genius, a money prophet and a money source.

Chapter 2

The Ultimate Energy

The world is a paradise of splendor. Abundance is our natural state of being. The supply of the Universe is limitless; therefore, your supply is limitless. You simply must tap into the limitless supply and then keep the supply flowing.

I must caution you before I reveal the exact science of attracting all good things, hence the exact science of attracting money, you need not understand "exactly how it works." You must, however, "have faith" that it does work and that it will work for you. Just think of all the things in your life that you don't fully understand yet work for you. I don't fully understand how electricity works, yet I have an unlimited supply of it. I don't fully understand how water flows into my home, yet all I have to do is turn on the faucet and out it flows.

You don't have to "figure out" every aspect of why these principles work. I urge you to put your ego aside during this process and just allow the principles to magically change your reality. You don't have to "work hard" to experience the full power of the Money Chi principles; you only have to believe they can and will work for you. Allow the Universe to work for you, expand for you and deliver gifts to you rather than believing you must "chase after" results. The faster you become "egoless" in this process, the faster your supply will be increased.

Principle 1. We are all creators of our own experiences.

The "stuff" occurring in our lives is merely a reflection of our thoughts, words, actions, beliefs and most importantly, *our feelings*. Most people don't allow money to flow into their lives because they don't **feel** they deserve it. They don't **feel** like they worked hard enough for it. Somehow, some way, they **feel** guilty about receiving or accepting money.

You MUST realize that your world can be limitless in all respects. It is sacrilegious to believe the Universe is built on principles of lack, deprivation or poverty. The Universe proves that premise false every moment of every day.

So the question arises "How do I change how I **feel** about money?" The answer: you change the way you **feel** about yourself. You must have faith in yourself. You must elevate and empower yourself. And actually, the process is quite simple (there is power in simplicity).

1. **Release all poverty consciousness.** Don't allow poverty to exist in your reality. You can't get poor enough to help the poor and you can't get sick enough to help the sick. You can create your own world of perfection. Focus your energy on attracting and accepting money. This does not mean you shouldn't help others. It means you must become powerful in your own right and then help others do the same. The world's wealthiest people are also the greatest philanthropists.

2. **Forgive yourself for ever abusing, manipulating or using money with a negative intention.** Remember, money isn't destructive. Our thoughts and actions create our money experience. Repeatedly say to yourself, "I forgive myself and others for any past negative money thoughts and actions." Then let your "guilt" go and move on.

3. **Replace any poverty thoughts, lack thoughts or limiting beliefs about money with the absolute belief that money is good.** One of the affirmations I use every day is "Money is good…Money is God in action." I refuse to believe there is anything negative about money, because there isn't anything negative about money. It's all good.

For more details on the use of affirmations and a series of exercises that can help you with this process, go to _www.themoneychi.com_. You will find many fun and simple ways to transmute any negative money thoughts into positive money attractors. You can also read _Your Spiritual Gold Mind – The Divine Guide To Financial Freedom._ This book contains in excess of 100 Money Affirmations to help you establish healthy and positive money paradigms.

Chapter 3

Forget About What You Need

"But I don't really ***need*** all that money." Forget about what you need and focus on what you intend to experience. "Need" is a word of lack and deprivation. If you **feel** you don't **need** money, you can send it to me. My address is at the end of this book. I promise you I will put it to **good** use.

Most people find creative ways to prevent money from flowing into their lives. One of those ways is by establishing a belief that they "only need" a limited amount. This belief is absolutely contrary to laws of the Universe. The Universe doesn't "need" to expand every day, but it does. We were born to make manifest the glory of God, and as Nelson Mandela so aptly put it, "Your playing small does not serve the world." You were born to create, to add value to the world and to expand in every way possible. You have an inherent birthright and genetic obligation to do so. In nature, all things are growing and expanding, if not, they are withering away. Nature abhors a vacuum. Stagnation, the unwillingness to experience our full potential, is simply a form of demise.

So you have a choice. You can expand and grow. You can add to a collective consciousness of expansion and prosperity or you can add to a collective consciousness of lack, limitation and demise. Whatever you choose, so shall your reality be.

Principle 2. Choose to expand. Choose to accept only what you desire. Never settle for anything less.

There is an unmistakable truth and an incredible enlightenment that every "money genius" has discovered: the Universe **always** conforms to our expectations. If we believe in and expect lack, guilt, greed or limitation, that's what we receive. If we believe in and expect an ever-increasing supply of money, abundance and opulence, that's what we receive. Just look at the ***Robb Report*** and you will see the possibilities.

Your mission, if you choose to *accept it*, is to establish a mental and physical standard of wealth and then allow the Universe to deliver it to you. Once the Universe begins to deliver opportunities your way to add value to the world, *accept the opportunities* and *accept the resulting prosperity*. This does not mean action is irrelevant. Taking action on our desires is a *form of acceptance.* The Quakers have a saying, "When you pray, move your feet." In other words, the Universe always conforms to your desires in a manner that will encourage and allow you to expand while adding value to the world in the manner that is most appropriate for you.

For example, you may be a great teacher and the Universe may deliver you an opportunity to add value to the world through a new teaching experience (I can hear you saying now, "Teachers don't make a lot of money." However, I know teachers who are multi-millionaires and I know teachers who live in poverty…the choice is theirs). Accept that new teaching experience and fully immerse yourself in the glory of it; your increase will soon follow. And so it is true of your chosen manner of adding value to the world: accept the opportunities with a prosperity consciousness and accept the resulting treasures.

Establish your expectations with a positive intention and belief that the Universe will conform to your expectations because the Universe always does. Set high standards for yourself, not in terms of how hard you will work for the money, but in terms of how willing you are to *accept only what it is you truly want to be, do and have in life.* Don't settle for anything less. There is simply no need to settle for anything less than what it is you really intend and desire.

Chapter 4

Become A Money Magnet
(It's All About The Money)

Why beat around the bush? The simple fact is, we live in a society where money is the main form of self-expression. Many people ask me why they can't seem to attract money. When I question them about how and what they think about money, what they ask for in prayer and meditation or what they affirm and visualize each day, virtually everyone tells me they ask for prosperity and abundance. Well, why not ask for money? When you ask the Universe, God, The Infinite Intelligence, The Source Of All, for prosperity and abundance, the Universe is puzzled. The Universe responds by stating, "Look around, you are surrounded by prosperity and abundance. You have unlimited resources, water, air, the beauty of nature, the oceans and mountains, food, clothing...the list goes on. You already have that which you seek."

If you intend to have money, *then ask the Universe for money!* Focus on money. Think about money. Surround yourself with people who have money. Put yourself in places where there is money. Raise your consciousness about money since money is the resource you truly desire.

Principle 3. Be specific with your intentions and expectations. Be clear and direct with your intentions.

With just this one principle, you can change your reality forever. You have a right to be a money magnet. You have a right to stake your claim to whatever you desire from the Universe. So, immerse yourself in money thoughts, money exercises and money actions. Play *The Money Chi Game* (this game is designed to increase your awareness and acceptance of money...as much money as you desire). Here are a few simple yet powerful steps to becoming a money magnet:

1. **You must accept the truth that money is good.** Affirm this belief every day: "Money is good...Money is God in Action."

2. **You must affirm and visualize the receipt of money.** Here are some of my favorite money affirmations (I am certain some of these affirmations were originally scribed by other people. If you see an affirmation below that sounds familiar, please let me know so I can give credit in subsequent writings to the original author of the affirmation. Over the years I have read and used hundreds of affirmations and I must admit I do not recall the source of all of them).

- I love money and money loves me. Money flows to me easily, effortlessly and continuously in ever-increasing amounts.
- I am a money magnet with the power within to attract an unlimited supply of money and I accept my supply NOW.
- I am a channel of the limitless money supply.
- I now accept all the money I desire for the good of all concerned.
- I now accept $1 Million dollars (or amount specific) or something better for the good of all concerned.
- I deserve to be wealthy.

For more extensive information on how to write and utilize affirmations, see _Affirmations Of Wealth – 101 Secrets Of Daily Success_ or _Your Spiritual Gold Mind – The Divine Guide To Financial Freedom._

1. **You must allow yourself to accept money.** Whenever anyone offers you money, accept it. Get in the habit of receiving money in all amounts for all reasons. Don't ever reject money regardless of the source (unless it is illegal of course).
2. **Be fearless in your expectation, attraction, acceptance and circulation of money.** As silly as this may sound, most people are afraid of money. Become fearless. Believe you expect and deserve the best from life. It makes no sense to hide in the dark when you can live in the light.

3. **Remain conscious of your ability to attract or repel money.**
   The law of attraction is absolute. What we believe, ***what we
   feel***, what we immerse ourselves in is what we attract. If you feel
   guilty about money, or if you feel you limit someone else's supply
   of money when you have more, then you will automatically repel
   money. If you feel good about money (feel good about yourself)
   and you have positive expectations, money will continue to flow
   your way.

Chapter 5

Continually Raise Your Money Vibration

We all have a money DNA, a predisposition to inherit the money traits, tendencies and beliefs of our parents. As we leave the nest, we tend to find friends with money beliefs that mirror our own. It is a fact that our income will roughly equal the income of the 10 people with whom we spend the most time. If you want to increase your income, invest more time with people who have a significantly higher income level than you do. You can raise your vibration (your money consciousness) to a whole new level, simply by associating with people who have more money!

Principle 4. Live every day as if it were a special occasion.

During holidays and special events, such as anniversaries, weddings and birthdays we all celebrate. I refer to these as the times when we "use the good china."

Why not live a life of opulence and magnificence every day? Take every opportunity, no matter how insignificant it may seem, to immerse yourself in luxury every day. Why not use your good china every day?

Several years ago, Lora, a client of mine, invited my wife and me to her winter home in Palm Beach during the height of the social season. She took us to her club, The Mar-a-Lago Club, a private club owned by Donald Trump with members who include some of the world's wealthiest people. At dinner one night, I looked around the room and observed the atmosphere. At every table, people were smiling and laughing, treating each meal as if it were a celebration. When Mr. Trump came into the room, he immediately added to the positive energy, greeting every member and guest with a joke or laughter. After dinner, I asked Lora about her lifestyle. After all, we ate our meals at the Mar-a-Lago Club or the Palm Beach Polo Club, attended evening socials and fundraisers where millions of dollars were donated to charity and shopped on famous Worth Avenue.

Lora's response was simple, direct and honest. She said, "John, this is the way life is supposed to be. Every day is an opportunity to celebrate, to immerse yourself in life's magnificence. I can't think of any reason not to do this." Interestingly, Lora is a self-made millionaire and a single mother of two. Her summer residence is in the Four Seasons Hotel & Condominiums in downtown Boston. Lora has developed a money consciousness that "allows" her to "accept" money wherever she is, no matter what she is doing. Her focus is plain and simple: she believes in living life at its highest standard. She refuses to allow anything less than opulence into her life. As a result, she experiences opulence every day.

Many times, when I tell that story to people who attend our seminars or participate in our coaching programs, they immediately respond by saying something like "I couldn't afford to do something like that." I then tell them the rest of the story. Lora not only hosted my wife and me for that week in Palm Beach, she also paid for the entire trip, including airfare and meals. She "treated" us to everything we experienced. That's because Lora fully understands the Money Chi Principles. She not only accepts and allows money into her life; she circulates it freely and *energizes her money with gratitude.* She is grateful for our friendship as am I. Experiencing that week of magnificence and opulence was simply the natural expression of our gratitude for each other and our belief in each other. *We had attained the same vibration (the same level of energy and understanding).* You have the ability to elevate your vibration as well. Recognize and appreciate people who have in life what you desire and raise yourself to their vibration.

Chapter 6

Be Gratitude

Of all The Money Chi principles, this is by far the most important... *Gratitude* is the fuel that makes the engine run; it *is the force that adds velocity to everything we are capable of being.* The best summation of the power of gratitude was expressed by Wallace D. Wattles in his landmark book, <u>*The Science Of Getting Rich.*</u> Mr. Wattles states:

*"You cannot exercise much power without gratitude because it is gratitude that keeps you connected with power. The creative power within us makes us into the image of that to which we give our attention. **The grateful mind is constantly fixed upon the best; therefore it will receive the best.**"*

Principle 5. Stake your claim to anything and everything you desire from life and give gratitude for it in advance.

Yes, I said, "give gratitude for it in advance." The most successful people I have ever met all understand this principle. The least understood, yet the most powerful money mindset, is this simple:

Make every decision about your life based on **what you want to experience,** not based on what you think you can afford. Once you make your decision, once you make your choice, **give gratitude to the Universe for its manifestation NOW. There** is no greater or more powerful way of displaying your faith and establishing your claim. **The instant you give gratitude for what you intend to be, do or have, every force in the Universe lines up on your side and begins the delivery process.** Your charge at this point is to **accept whatever it is to which you have staked your claim.**

Sure it is wonderful to give gratitude for what you currently have, for the blessings you have already received. However, that places focus on what you already have. What about the person you expect to be? What about the unrealized dreams? What about the things you expect to have?

Become a walking, breathing, acting force of gratitude. The most powerful way to stake your claim to anything (and increase its velocity) is to give gratitude for it now.

Here is a sample gratitude affirmation for you:

I am so grateful I am becoming a debt free multi-millionaire. Source Of All, Thank You.

Chapter 7

Get Out Of Your Own Way

For may people, this is the most difficult principle to implement. Once you have decided what you expect from life. After you have decided to create your own reality, to elevate your vibration and to give gratitude for all the magnificence coming your way, *you must allow it to happen.*

At this point virtually everyone says to me, "Of course I am going allow it to happen. This is what I have been hoping for my entire life." Unfortunately most people get to this point and then deny themselves every amazing pleasure to which they are entitled. Why does this happen? Why do most people get to the verge of the fulfillment of every desire they have ever dreamed of and then deny themselves the very satisfaction they allege they want? The answer is simple, but not simplistic…most people have never experienced the true fulfillment of their desires. They get within a millimeter or a millisecond of the greatest experience of their lives and they begin to doubt their worthiness to receive it.

Principle 6. You deserve to be wealthy. You deserve to be happy. You deserve every unbridled pleasure available. Therefore, you must get out of your own way and allow yourself to accept it.

This is a scary proposition for most people. After all, what are people going to think of me when I am rich? Do I really deserve to have it all? I'll have to pay so much more in taxes. Won't I be taking something away from someone else? Maybe they need it more than I do. What am I going to do? I changed my mind; I don't really want everything I said I wanted.

STOP!

You must have the courage to truly fulfill your desires and your destiny. Remember, you have a universal mandate to expand, to grow and to prosper.

You deserve to be wealthy. You were born to make manifest the glory of God. You are a child of God and *your playing small does not serve the world.* Accept your bounty. When you do, the entire Universe prospers.

Chapter 8

Keep It Flowing

At this point, you have learned to create your money life by design. You have learned to stay focused on attracting and receiving money. You have learned to give gratitude in advance for money and you have learned how to allow yourself to accept money. Now you will learn the importance of circulating money.

Principle 7. Our money must always be in circulation or it becomes stale and loses its velocity (its energy).

When we circulate money, we circulate ourselves, our energy and our intentions. If we "hoard" money or treat it with disrespect, we block the flow of money circulating in our individual economy. This is not to say we shouldn't save or invest money. Keep in mind, when we are investing money, we are putting it to use. We are investing our energy and intentions in people, products and services that are adding value to the world.

One of the most successful real estate agents in the US is a middle-aged Japanese American woman who was taught many years ago to "bless" her money. When Keiko circulates money, she passes on her positive intentions for prosperity to other people. Keiko takes a moment when she signs each check or hands over currency to another and she "impresses" the money with her energy, her positive expectations, her desire that the money will multiply "for the good of all concerned." It is no wonder Keiko is a multi-millionaire and her income and net-worth increase constantly. Keiko sent me an email this week telling me about all the fantastic investments and sales she is making (she purchased three new investment properties, sold two million dollar homes and listed two new properties for sale as an agent). She then added that each of these things happened with *"only a few phone calls."*

Another "amazing" thing to know about this story is that the real estate market in her area is "down significantly." When I speak with

Keiko however, she *never* acknowledges what others perceive as a "down market." She only sees opportunity and ways to add value to the world through her intentions and her actions. Keiko is 100% focused on creating her own reality, and the Universe delivers every time. She continues to circulate her money and her blessings. The reason Keiko will increase her net worth to approximately $50 Million in the next few years is because she refuses to stop the flow. Most people "in a down market" pull in the reigns. They run for safety. They "save for a rainy day."

But there are no rainy days in Keiko's mind. The sun is always shining and the money is always flowing.

Chapter 9

You Are Home

In my 20 years of interviewing and working with extraordinarily successful people, I have learned many fascinating and empowering principles. Although it may sound like a cliché, the truth is, the answers and solutions to every challenge or opportunity lie within you. The answers aren't "out there." The circumstances occurring in our lives are an exact reflection of our thoughts, words, actions, beliefs and feelings. Even though it may not seem it, the only things we have complete control of are our thoughts, words, actions, beliefs and feelings. Many of us want to make excuses, play the victim and seek sympathy for the way the world treats us. The solution is simple. Take control of your own life. Tap into the vital essence that is stored deep within you. Raise your vibration to the level of magnificence you are entitled to experience.

Let's review The Money Chi Principles:

1. **We are all creators of our own experiences.** The awesome extension of this principle is that we can deliberately create our own experiences. You have the right and the power to be, do and have whatever you expect to experience from life. The Universe is your playground. It's your canvas, ready to be painted.

2. **Choose to expand. Choose to accept only what you desire. Never settle for anything less.** There is absolutely no reason to ever settle for anything less than what you desire. It is as easy to attract a 5,000 square foot house as it is to attract a 2,000 square foot house. The Universe doesn't differentiate between $100 and $1 Million. Expand your thinking and accept only what you truly intend to experience. The Universe will deliver. It must deliver.

3. **Be specific, clear and direct with your intentions and expectations.** If you expect money, *ask for money*. Be specific in your petition to the Universe. You already live in a world of

abundance and prosperity. The Universe has already supplied you with all the abundance and prosperity you require. *Ask for money* and *accept money* when it flows your way. Use money affirmations and remember to always add the words "or something better," when you stake your claim i.e., "I now accept $1 Million dollars or something better for the good of all concerned."

4. **Live every day as if it were a special occasion.** Use the fine china every day. Wear your "Sunday Best" every day. *Raise your vibration* to your expectations. Constantly put yourself in places and with people who have attained what you desire.

5. **Stake your claim to anything and everything you desire from life and <u>give gratitude for it in advance</u>.** Make every decision about your life based on what you want to experience, not based on what you think you can afford. Once you make your decision, once you make your choice, give gratitude to the Universe for its manifestation *NOW*. There is no greater or more powerful way of displaying your faith and establishing your claim. The instant you give gratitude for what you intend to be, do or have, every force in the Universe lines up on your side and begins the delivery process. Your charge at this point is to accept whatever it is you have staked your claim to.

6. **You deserve to be wealthy. You deserve to be happy. You deserve every unbridled pleasure available. Therefore, you must get out of your own way and <u>allow yourself to accept it.</u>** You were born to make manifest the glory of God. You are a child of God and your playing small does not serve the world. Accept your bounty. When you do, the entire Universe prospers.

7. **Our money must always be in circulation or it becomes stale and loses its velocity (its energy).** When we circulate money, we circulate ourselves, our energy and our intentions. Keep your money flowing (with your blessings and positive intentions) and it will pick up energy and return to you multiplied many times over

Chapter 10

What Do I Do Next?

At this point, many of you are saying, "Okay, I understand the principles, but how do I apply them in my life?" Everyone has a different recipe for success, however the main ingredients are all the same. Every morning just after you wake and every evening just before you go to sleep, put the "main ingredients" of your money recipe to work for you. I suggest the following:

1. Affirmations & Visualization. Not your average affirmations. Use your money specific affirmations. See our *website* for more suggestions. It is helpful to do this with a partner.
2. Money Meditations. There are several money meditations and other recommendations at our *website*. Twenty minutes a day of money meditations is perfect. If you prefer, you can use Wayne Dyer's Meditations For Manifesting.
3. Play *The Money Chi Game*. There is no better way to create the habit of receiving money than playing this game. It is easy, fun and incredibly powerful. A few minutes a week is all it takes.
4. Join a Money Chi *Millionaire Mastermind Group* or find a way to raise your vibration to Millionaire status. Put yourself in places where millionaires socialize, do business or play. Soak in the atmosphere; breathe in the "richness."
5. Experiment and tell us what works for you. We will post your results to the website and with your permission, we'll report your success on our Millionaire Mastermind and Money Chi Game conference calls.

Chapter 11

It's The Law

In my previous book, *Your Spiritual Gold Mind-The Divine Guide To Financial Freedom,* I set out several Money Laws. The money awareness laws are specific principles that affect our consciousness and awareness of money, how we receive it, how we circulate it, what it represents to us and how much we have of it. These concise laws will raise your consciousness (and thus your vibration) about money to a much higher level.

The Law Of Familiarity.

We tend to inherit the traits, tendencies, attitudes and beliefs of our parents about money.

We each have a "money heritage" or genealogy that can last for generations. We each also create the future money heritage of our families. We instill both our conscious and unconscious money beliefs in our children. Our children absorb our money "actions" as well. As a result of years of conditioning, our children tend to follow in our financial footsteps.

Recommendation: Analyze your current savings, income and debt levels. Think back to when your parents were your age and try to recall (or ask them) what their savings, income and debt levels were. After adjusting for inflation, you may find your savings, income and debt levels, in terms of adjusted dollars, are within a few percentage points of your parents. Make up your mind today to establish the money heritage you want to pass on to your children, grandchildren and extended family. Then, do it.

The Law Of Consciousness.

The more awareness we have when saving, earning, investing or circulating money, the more money we have.

When we lose consciousness about money because of an addiction, the method we use to spend money or indifference toward money, the less we have. Always stay conscious and aware of money in all forms. Money will tend to respond to your consciousness. If you have total awareness of your sources of income, money opportunities and the flow of money in your life, you generate and keep much more of it.

Recommendation: When you spend or circulate money today, stop and look at the dollar (or whatever denomination) bills you are spending. Stop and think about why you are letting the money out of your life and ask yourself, "Is this a good investment?" Always stop and think before you spend. If you use a credit (debt) card or electronic commerce of any type, picture or visualize the cash leaving your hands as you make the purchase. This will help you realize how much money you are actually spending.

The Law Of Responsibility.

Be responsible with your money.

If you have thoughts, such as, "well its only money," you are indicating a tendency to be irresponsible with it. Do the "little things" right with your money. If you are owed change from a purchase and it is "only a penny," don't walk away from it and leave it there. That is disrespectful. Deposit your money in the highest yielding accounts, even if the interest rate is only slightly higher. Call your credit (debt) card company and ask them to lower your interest rate. When you are responsible with (and to) your money, your money will respond accordingly.

Recommendation: Take all of your "loose change" and deposit it into your investment or savings account. Start earning interest on it. This is just one way to train your subconscious mind to respect money and to train your money to respect you. Be creative. I am sure you can think of several more ways to accomplish this as well.

The Law Of Regeneration.

In order to generate more money, we need to regenerate ourselves.

This is done through prayer, affirmation, visualization, love and gratitude. Refer back to The Money Chi principles for more insight on this. We must clear ourselves of past negative money experiences and fears in order to generate and keep money in our lives.

Recommendation: Write down your most compelling money fears. Writing them down on a piece of paper will help you "release your fears." Then develop an affirmation, or use one of the Affirmations at our *website*, to help you release this fear.

The Law Of Simplicity.

The simpler we keep our lives, the simpler it is to attract money.

Many of us tend to complicate our lives as some sort of "justification" mechanism. We tend to make things much more difficult than they need to be as some sort of test of our worthiness. Forget about this and simplify. If you use so much time and energy keeping your life complicated, you won't have the energy left to invest in making or attracting money, wealth or love into your life. Keep things simple and you will have more money.

Recommendation: Write down one way you can simplify your life today. Decide to "uncomplicate" your life by finding the simplest way to get things done.

The Law Of Attraction.

Money is attracted to people who have awareness of, respect for and discipline when using it.

We each can become "money magnets" by changing our awareness, our thoughts and attitudes, and by willingly accepting or assuming responsibility in our lives. Money tends to flow to people who have abundant and prosperous thoughts, who take prosperous actions, and who render service with or out of love. The "money chase" can be over for you if you change your attitude.

Recommendation: You can begin attracting money into your life today. Visualize money (currency) flowing into your home, business and accounts. Give thanks to God for the good you have received. In a short period of time, if you use the other recommendations in this book, money will flow to you naturally.

The Law Of Acceptance.

In order to have more money, we must be willing to accept it.

Many people get caught up in continually "denying" money. If someone offers you money, even if they are close friends or family members, graciously and gratefully accept it.

Recommendation: Practice accepting and receiving gifts. Literally practice. Ask a friend to come to your house. Tell them about this book and that you are training your subconscious mind to be comfortable receiving money. Have them hand you money (cash) over and over. Keep taking the money and practice receiving it. This may seem silly, but this is a powerful way to build up your willingness to accept and attract money.

The Law Of Discipline.

Financial discipline is the surest path to financial freedom. Proper budgeting, investing and appreciation of our money is one of the most liberating experiences in our spiritual and financial lives.

When we are disciplined with anything, we eventually have more of it. Think about this for a moment. The more disciplined we are with our time, the more time we have. The more disciplined we are with our eating and exercise habits, we have longer, healthier, more abundant lives. The same principle holds true in every aspect of our lives. When we are disciplined with our money, the more we have.

Recommendation: You intuitively know what you must do here.

The Law Of Observation.

Always keep your money in sight. If you lose sight of your money, you will forget about it. *When we forget about money, it forgets about us and tends to take on a life of its own.* Those of you who have teenagers know what I mean. If you have a stock portfolio, check it every day.

If you have account books, physically pick them up and look at them periodically. If you have cash in your home, keep it where you can physically see it or check on it regularly. Keep in mind, these are money "awareness" laws. In order to build financial wealth and the ability to attract money, we must train our subconscious to do so.

Recommendation: If you have Internet access, build a stock portfolio and check it twice a day. You can do this with almost any "on-line" service. If you don't have Internet access, read the financial section of the newspaper today or subscribe to The Wall Street Journal. Make some "imaginary" stock picks and track them every day. Take out your bank books or investment statements. Arrange them neatly, free from clutter and confusion. Each morning and evening, look at them (or check them on-line).

The Law Of Maturity.

Spiritual maturity leads to financial and investment maturity.

The more mature or "grown-up" we are, the more our money "grows." If we are immature in our thinking and our spiritual commitments, the less likely we are to gain financial independence.

Recommendation: Write down one way you can "mature" spiritually. What commitment can you make to "grow up" spiritually? Make this commitment and watch your money grow.

The Law Of Indebtedness.

If we are spiritually, emotionally or physically indebted to anyone or anything, we tend to become financially indebted; our debt levels tend to be high or unmanageable. This happens, in many instances, due to a feeling of inadequacy, lack of self-worth (unworthiness) or guilt. I see this very often in family-owned businesses. If parents own a business for many years and pass it on to their children, who don't really want to be a part of it, the children tend to have very high debt levels, spiritually, emotionally, physically and financially. Out of a sense of "loyalty" to their parents or family heritage, the children stay in the business only to develop low self-esteem because they know deep down inside they would rather be doing something else. This is a cycle that continues to perpetuate feelings of guilt, and as a result, more debt.

Debts also tend to grow in our lives when we don't use cash. As simple as this seems, most people lose awareness of how much they are spending and continue to increase their debt as a result. Use cash as much as possible in your financial transactions.

Debts can also develop as a result of the "mental bank accounts" we keep. We all tend to keep track physically of the "favors" we have done for people. We then "expect" them to do the same in return. If they don't, we get upset. Forget about keeping mental bank accounts, they are another form of debt accumulation. If you can't do this, start paying cash for "friendly" favors.

Recommendation: Write down everything you "feel guilty about." List these items on a piece of paper. Then write how each item may have affected your financial life and "let them all go."

The Law Of Replenishment.

People who have a sense of giving, who continually give responsibly of their money to causes important to them, tend to attract more money into their lives. This is because we each can be an outlet of both love and energy. *People who "give" with no expectation of anything in return or "tithe" with the intention of replenishing the source of their money, make great investments of love.* We can each be great philanthropists in our own way no matter how much money we give or tithe. Give and tithe money out of a sense of gratitude, love and glorification of God, not out of a sense of duty or obligation (this is just another form of psychic debt). When you give with gratitude and love, you open the channels for great abundance.

Recommendation: Take the money out of your pockets right now. Take 10% of it and give it to a cause or charity that has a special meaning or   sentiment for you. Even if this is only $1.00, give it with love. The love you will receive in return will be plentiful. Don't wait...do this now!

The Law Of Enthusiasm.

The word enthusiasm means "one with the energy of God," or "the God within." When we earn, invest and multiply our money with enthusiasm, we are doing so in a godlike manner. Genuine enthusiasm (not the phony stuff we see and hear so often), displays a genuine love for God, love for what we are doing and love for other people. *When we are one with the energy of God, we are spiritually connected to everyone and everything. God is all encompassing, and so can you be. Be genuinely enthusiastic about the divine plan of your life and follow it faithfully. By so doing, you will automatically be filled with the energy of God, in all forms, including money.*

Recommendation: Write down all the things that get you enthusiastic or the things for which you show great enthusiasm. Then ask yourself, "How can I convert my enthusiasm to profit?" Listen for the answer, then do it.

The Law Of Gratitude.

Of all the money awareness laws, I believe this is the most important. Developing and maintaining an attitude of gratitude about everything in our lives leads to the "flood gates opening."

If you have a job you hate, remember you have this job as a result of your own choices. Give thanks that you have a job and a source of income. Continue to give gratitude and your attitude will change. Soon after, new opportunities will arise and new doors will open. Give thanks for those as well, then seize them and make them a real part of your life. Your gratitude for the good that you have will always lead to more good in the future.

Recommendation: Verbally tell someone today you are grateful for their contribution to your life, then thank God as well. Make this a habit then watch the floodgates open.

The Law Of Circulation.

Our money must always be in circulation or it becomes stale and loses its energy.

When we circulate money, we circulate ourselves, our energy and our intentions. If we "hoard" money or treat it with disrespect, we block the flow of money circulating in our individual spiritual economies. Now this is not to say we shouldn't save or invest money. Keep in mind, when we are investing money, we are putting it to use. We are investing our energy, love and intentions in people and products that are hopefully doing the same thing (perpetuating this energy). *Keep circulating your money through responsible spending, loving charity and spiritually mature investment decisions. Then your money will "pick up energy" and return to you multiplied.*

Recommendation: Write down the last time you experienced a "money blockage" and why you think you had this experience. Could you have avoided this through proper money circulation? How?

The Law Of Belief.

When our money travels, it takes with it our beliefs, attitudes and intentions. We literally "impress our mentality" onto our money and send our mentality to other people and places.

This is a very important point. Always be aware of your attitude when releasing or circulating money. Whatever your attitude is, at the time you release (spend, give, invest) money, will have a dramatic effect on the results it will generate in the future. If you have thoughts of limitation at the time you release money, you will produce limitation in multiples for yourself and probably for other people. If you have thoughts of genuine enthusiasm, love, hope, charity and abundance when releasing money, you will produce the same in multiples as well. Remember, nature always compensates in multiples.

Recommendation: Think about your day today. When you released money, what was your attitude? If your attitude was negative, change it now. "Re-send" thoughts of abundance and prosperity to the recipients of your money. If your thoughts while releasing money today were positive, congratulations. Nature will reward you.

The Law Of Love.

Bless your money, the Source of it, and the recipients of it, with love. Give with love, invest with love, circulate with love and you will have love in great returns. You may not understand yet. I mean literally bless it. Make up a short blessing or prayer of love, prosperity and abundance. Send this spiritual message with your money, checks, etc., by reciting it when releasing money. *When we bless our money, we endow, consecrate or sanctify the receiver of it.*

I also recommend you keep your money (the cash, checks, etc., that you keep at home) in a blessed or sacred place. Where is the most spiritual place in your home? Prepare a place for your money there. *Keep aware, this is not to worship your money; I do not recommend idolatry in any form.* You want your money in a blessed or sacred place so it will carry blessings with it wherever it goes.

Recommendation: Develop one way you can pass on your love with your money. Put this into action today.

By now, your awareness of money and the various means of manifesting financial wealth may be starting to shift. As you practice the money awareness laws, you will become one with the consciousness of God in all aspects of your life, including your financial life. Your spiritual economy is beginning to take shape. You have all the tools necessary for financial freedom. Now go mine some gold!

The Money Application Laws

Now that you are "aware" of what money really is and how it acts and reacts in your life, you are ready to mine some gold. The money application laws are specific financial planning and manifestation principles that have been proven in the financial marketplace for years. In this section, you are going to learn how to apply these principles "in the real world" to garner specific financial gains.

The Receiving (commonly referred to as the "Earning") Laws.

1. *Receive money honestly and with integrity.* If you "earn" money disingenuously, you will build up a force of negative energy that may impair you spiritually and financially.

2. *Do what you love and love what you do.* If you love your profession, love will spill over into every area of your life. Conversely, if you hate your job or profession, hate will spill over into every other area of your life. You must have the courage to live your dreams and live them now. Develop a responsible transition plan to follow your dreams; your dreams will eventually follow you.

3. *Money can and should "flow" to you from many different sources.* Income should "stream" to you as natural as a flowing river. There is a profession, career, investment(s) and/or opportunities within your subconscious (gold) mind right now that will allow this to happen. Tap into your *gold mind* and put your ideas into action.

4. *Get in the habit of continuously receiving money whether you believe you "earned it" or not.* This money is flowing to you for a good reason.

5. *Always think and act like an entrepreneur.* Everyone is self-employed. Make yourself "invaluable" to your company and/or your clients and customers (and make no mistake about it, everyone is your customer). Go the extra mile in everything you do and do it with genuine enthusiasm. Every entrepreneur takes "ownership" in her company. You must do the same.

The "Savings" Laws.

1. *Money cannot save you, but you can save money.* Don't think of accumulating financial wealth as "savings." Think of it as an investment.

2. *Invest the maximum allowable by law in your 401k, 403b or similar investment plan.* If you are self-employed, establish a profit sharing or simplified retirement plan and pay yourself first. Contribute to this plan every month. It doesn't matter at first what the amount is; developing the habit of doing this is what counts.

3. *Save money regularly.* Aim for 10% of your after tax-income or more (again, only if you have no credit card debt. If you have credit card debt, make it your top financial priority to pay that off first). If you don't think you have the money, cut your expenses. This is a matter of priority.

4. *Have money direct deposited from your "paycheck" directly into an investment or savings account.* You won't miss what you don't see.

5. *Establish IRA (these should be called ILAs – Individual Living Accounts NOT Individual Retirement Accounts) accounts for your children immediately.* When your children begin to work, they can begin making contributions. Teach your children the importance and discipline of saving and investing from the earliest age possible. The sooner you start, the easier this will be.

6. *Use time to your advantage.* Time has value and the time value of money is astounding. Stop wasting time and start investing your time and money now.

7. *Do not try to save money in your checking account.* Think about this logically for a moment. When money goes into your checking account, what is it actually doing? It is waiting to be spent! Deposit all your money into a savings or investment account. Only transfer money to your checking account when necessary to pay bills or to make large purchases when cash is not practical.

Chapter 12

Commencement Day

What a wonderful word, commencement. It is a word typically associated with graduating. And, in a sense, that is what you have done by completing this book. However, Commencement Day is also a day of new beginnings, anticipation and positive expectations for the future.

Remember, the answers to all of your questions aren't "out there." Your search is over. You have attracted The Money Chi principles because it was your destiny to do so. Your intentions brought you here and now you realize every answer to every question, every solution to every challenge, every means to every end lies within you. You have the innate power and ability to not only dream grand dreams, but to realize them.

It is not a matter of conquering your fears or defeating your challenges. You must simply allow the greatness that is within you (and it is within all of us) to reveal itself. Your true essence is magnificence. Your true calling is to make glory of everything you are and everything you do. Let your light shine.

Your playing small does not serve the world, so from this moment forward…allow yourself to "play big."

Contact Information

V. John Alexandrov
c/o Legacy Capital Solutions, LLC
10 Chestnut Street – Suite 640
Worcester, MA 01608

Websites

www.themoneychi.com
www.legacycapitalsolutions.com

Email
johna@themoneychi.com

General Questions

info@themoneychi.com

Media Partner – Website Administration

Asagio Media Interactive, Inc.
67 Millbrook Street – Suite 113
Worcester, MA 01606

www.asagiomedia.com

AFFIRMATIONS OF *W*EALTH

101 Secrets Of Daily Success

V. John Alexandrov

YOUR PROGRAM
FOR SUCCESS

YOUR PROGRAM FOR SUCCESS

The purpose of this book is to help you develop a positive mind-set to achieve success in all areas of your life. Unfortunately, we are exposed to negative thinking every day... on our jobs, in the media, and in the words and actions of the people we meet. This negative thinking has a profound impact on how we perceive ourselves and what we become. Every truly successful person who discovers his or her inner strength, who achieves great things, does so with a positive frame of mind. A positive mental attitude can be developed and maintained by following the process revealed to you in this book. Without a doubt, to accomplish any goal you need to develop the proper mind-set. Confidence, which is cultivated through applied faith, can be an acquired virtue. It is a well established fact that repetition of thought in the form of daily affirmations or convictions will dramatically increase self-confidence. Upon acquiring the confidence necessary to take actions on your dreams and desires, you are well on the way to accomplishing any goal or fulfilling any mission.

I am Fearless ™

*T*HE MEANING OF WORDS

Throughout this book, you will see several familiar terms which have different meanings in the context of this writing than in everyday usage. These terms and their definitions are explained below.

1. *Applied Faith:*

Applied faith is faith coupled with action. In other words, faith is not faith at all unless you take the physical actions necessary to confirm it. Many people confuse faith with dreams, desires and beliefs. Faith is one step beyond. True faith, applied faith, is the courage to take action on your dreams, desires and beliefs, regardless of the consequences. It is a faith in yourself and in your God that is unshakable. Applied faith is the cornerstone of all great accomplishments and of the realization of all your dreams.

2. *Wealth:*

When most people think of wealth, they think of money, lavish homes and material riches. Wealth, as it is described here, is much more than that. Wealth is a state of mind, a manner of being. There are many people in this world who are rich with material possessions, but never become wealthy because they have not achieved the balance in their lives necessary to gain true wealth. Wealth is a balance of physical and mental health, spiritual fulfillment, love, family happiness, true friendships, social kindness and responsibility, the receipt and development of wisdom through knowledge and understanding, plus monetary success. If this balance is not achieved, and success is not accomplished in all areas of one's life, then true wealth can rarely be attained. While reading the affirmations in this book and writing your own, do not be singular in your interpretation and understanding of wealth. Keep in mind that wealth is a healthy balance of all the essential areas of your life.

3. Wisdom:

There is a definition of wisdom contained in one of the affirmations I have written, which reads, "Wisdom is the true understanding of one's purpose and mission in life, the recognition of one's God-given talents and the use of these talents to learn, to teach and to mentor others for the greater good of our fellow man."

When I developed this definition of wisdom, I was acutely aware of the responsibility we all have not only to learn and teach, but to do so for a greater good. We all have talents that God has given us. They were given to us to create a benefit for ourselves and for others. Wisdom is an understanding; it is the insight we gain from others and the awareness we develop from the discovery of our true mission and purpose in our lives. We all have a calling, a purpose, that we must pursue to utilize fully the latent talents that we each possess. The discovery, development, and utilization of these talents in the most prolific manner possible is the essence of wisdom.

4. God:

This book is not intended to be a "religious" philosophy. I have no desire to push a certain religious philosophy. We all have a spirituality about us, a spirit within us. There is no denying that there is an intelligence in this world that is much greater than us. We were created from this intelligence and we continue to be part of this intelligence every day. My personal beliefs are that there is a God, and we have received the gift of eternal life from the Lord Jesus Christ. Your beliefs may be different, but the basic nature of this book and the fundamental principles of my affirmations are temporal. I refer to God many times in my affirmations because these are my affirmations and they are important to me and to my development. My personal belief is that God has created me to serve you through the gifts I was granted. You may call your God something else, and you may believe in specific religious principles. If so, develop your affirmations around those principles, similar to the way I have developed my affirmations around my beliefs.

$\mathscr{S}$TEPS TO SUCCESS

Attaining wealth is a natural process. There are several steps to attaining true and total wealth. These steps are outlined below:

1. You must discover or create your true mission and purpose in life.

In other words, you must discover, develop and then utilize your God-given talents to their fullest. For many people this means finally pursuing a career, dream or goal they previously were conditioned to think was not achievable. For many people this means pursuing their own definition of success, rather than pursuing the definition they were influenced to believe by someone else. Whatever it may be, we all instinctively know what our true calling is. We have an obligation to ourselves to discover that true calling and to pursue it with the passion necessary to make it a reality.

2. You must apply your faith to your mission.

In my definition of applied faith, applying your faith to your mission means you must develop faith in yourself and in your mission to the point that you take the physical actions necessary to realize your dreams. In other words, with applied faith, you stop dreaming and wishing and start doing. This step takes confidence and courage. The development and repetition of your daily affirmations will reinforce your determination.

3. You must develop a written plan.

Almost all goals are achieved after a written plan is developed.

Sample goal planning-mission sheets can be found starting on page 242.

Any type of wealth may be achieved faster and more assuredly once you have crystallized your thoughts in writing.

4. You must develop the confidence to carry out your faith regardless of the circumstances, adversities or negative reactions of others.

Most people fear change, even if they are not making the changes. When you make up your mind and develop the necessary confidence to convert your dreams to reality, there will be many people who will try to stop you. Your confidence will reveal their insecurities. Your faith will uncover their lack of faith. Because of basic human nature, other people will try to hold you back. You must have the strength and courage to overcome their criticism. When you do so, you will be ready for any success and all the wealth you desire.

5. You must use your God-given talents to help other people.

You cannot develop total wealth unless you share your talents. When you share your talents, you help other people, and when you help other people, you are always rewarded.

6. You must aspire to achieve physical, spiritual and mental health.

Achieving a healthy balance in all areas of our lives is a fundamental step in the development of wealth.

7. You must utilize fully the power of your subconscious mind.

We each have a conscious and subconscious mind that can be developed to achieve great things. We are conditioned to believe that we have limitations, but our subconscious mind does not acknowledge limitations. Our subconscious mind believes anything that we tell it and, as a result, we can develop and utilize the astonishing untapped resources of our minds. Affirmation and visualization are two tools that help us fully use the power of our subconscious minds. As you will see, this power can and will be used to bring you whatever you want in life.

8. You must attain wisdom through learning experiences and understanding.

Wisdom is a foundation of wealth. Wisdom is developed over time and is an ongoing process. The development of wisdom is a journey. One basic fact we must acknowledge is that we need to let go of ego to gain wisdom. Wisdom is an understanding of our purpose and our calling and the development of our talents to pursue this calling.

9. You must share your wisdom and wealth with others for the greater good of your fellow man.

If you cannot share your wealth for the benefit of others, true wealth will not be granted to you. No matter how hard you try, no matter how much money you accumulate, if you cannot share your wealth, you will not be spiritually fulfilled or mentally healthy. Sharing your wisdom, and thereby your wealth, unlocks the door to total wealth.

THE POWER OF WORDS

In addition to the steps outlined above, spiritual or healing music greatly enhances physical, mental and spiritual health, while providing the clarity of thought necessary to seize opportunities when they are presented to you. I recommend that you listen to the music listed on pages 258 and 259 when you write your goals and affirmations and when you read your daily affirmations.

The affirmations presented in this book are my daily affirmations. I live each one of these affirmations every day. The power of self-developed affirmations, along with clearly defined written goals and applied faith, is unlimited. I use the term "self-developed" because, without a doubt, the most effective affirmations are those that you compose yourself.

For an affirmation to be truly effective, it should be self-written, you must believe in it, and it should have a profound emotional impact on you. Remember, "All things are possible to those that believe them." You must believe what you are affirming is possible. The instant you believe something is possible, it becomes probable. This is a very important point. If you lack the basic belief that what you are affirming is possible, your affirmation(s) will not work. Believe in yourself. The desires and dreams you have in your mind are the seeds of possibility and ultimately will become reality. The emotional aspect of each affirmation should not and cannot be overlooked. When you can "feel" your affirmations, as well as read or speak them, the impact and effectiveness of your affirmations increases dramatically.

Your written affirmations (and your goals) must spark an emotional response from you or they simply will not be effective.

You will notice that every affirmation I have written is composed in the present tense. This is very important. When written in the present tense, your subconscious mind will believe that you already are what you affirm. Since your subconscious mind already believes what you affirm, it will bring to you what you have affirmed. In other words, you will perform the physical acts necessary to live what you affirm or you will create the circumstances for them to be delivered to you.

You will also see that many of the affirmations and accompanying narrations contain the words "1 am." These are two of the most powerful words you can use when writing an affirmation. Again, you are what you believe. Therefore, if you compose an affirmation with the words "1 am," you will soon be what you believe.

The following affirmations demonstrate the power of the phrase "I am":

- I am successful.
- I am the spiritual person God intended me to be.
- I am an internationally recognized author and speaker.
- I am a loving husband and father.
- I am the leading salesperson in my company.

Another significant point to remember when developing

your affirmations is to write them in the positive tense. When many people begin to write their own affirmations, they write them in the negative tense, and therefore they defeat the effectiveness and purpose of the affirmation. Here are some "negatively" written affirmations:

- I will not have any fears today.
- I will not eat chocolate cake anymore.
- I will not be late for work.

Negatively written affirmations never work. When you try to convince yourself not to repeat a certain behavior (deny yourself), rather than affirm a positive result (give yourself positive reinforcement), you continue to think in the negative, and your affirmations become self-defeating. When you accentuate the positive in your affirmations, you naturally and automatically begin shifting your mind-set from negative thinking to positive thinking. Now lets compare the three "negative" affirmations to three "positive" affirmations:

- I am fearless.
- I am slim, healthy and ever-improving.
- I am prompt, alert and ready for work.

I think it is easy to see that the "positive affirmations" are certainly more motivational and encouraging. Your mind will naturally embrace any positively written affirmation and therefore, your physical actions will soon reflect your beliefs.

Remember, accentuate the positive, and eliminate the negative. Give yourself positive reinforcement every day and you will be well on your way to achieving success.

TIME FRAME

How long does it take for an affirmation to convince your subconscious mind to act upon what you affirm? I have read material that states as little as six days of repetition will have a dramatic affect on your self-confidence. However, from personal experience, I am convinced it takes 30 consecutive days of affirmation and continued affirmation *thereafter, as* necessary, for your mind to be convinced of what you affirm. There is no doubt, after 30 days of affirmation, you will see and feel a dramatic difference in your self-confidence, self-reliance and faith in yourself. You will begin to live what you affirm if you haven't already. This method never fails. Some people fail to exercise the self-discipline necessary to implement this method, but when kept to for 30 days, it never fails.

THE WRITTEN WORD

Another important factor in convincing your subconscious mind that you are what you affirm, is not only to read your affirmation aloud with belief and conviction for 30 days, but to write it 10 times a day as well. When writing an affirmation, you tend to focus more on the content and impact of the affirmation than if you only read the affirmation. Also, when writing an affirmation 10 times a day, you invoke the tactile sense of writing. Since you are writing the affirmation, you not only visualize the affirmation, but you can feel it as well because the pen or pencil is physically in your hands. This adds to the emotional impact of the affirmation.

In the next section, you will find a checklist of questions you need to ask yourself before developing your affirmations. This checklist is actually a self-discovery tool, which will assist you in focusing on the areas most important to you. This checklist will make you stop, think and reflect on your life, your desires and your dreams.

After each affirmation there is a section for you to make personal notes about the affirmation. In the *Thoughts* section, write the feelings, emotions and thoughts that run through your mind while reading each affirmation. Carefully and consciously consider your answers to the checklist questions and your personal notes before writing your own affirmations. In the *Actions* section, list the actions you need to take to make your dreams, desires, thoughts, goals and affirmations a reality. Describe in detail the physical actions you will take to put your affirmations in motion. Remember, "faith without action is dead." You can use my affirmations as a guide to assist you when necessary. I have developed the 101 affirmations you are about to read. The number of affirmations you develop is up to you. There is no magic number.

*S*UMMARY FOR SUCCESS

Keep in mind the following steps as your guide:

1. Complete the self-discovery checklist in the next section and review your personal notes and Thoughts before writing your affirmations.

2. Write your affirmations in the present tense.

3. Use the words "I am" whenever appropriate.

4. Listen to the spiritual music when developing, writing and reading your affirmations.

5. Repeat your affirmations, verbally and in writing, for a period of 30 consecutive days for the full impact of your affirmations to take hold. Repetition of your affirmations is essential to your success. I write my newly developed affirmations 10 times a day and repeat them aloud several times per day. After 30 days, continue to affirm your beliefs and desires verbally whenever possible (preferably every day).

6. Evoke as much emotion as possible when writing and verbalizing your affirmations. You must believe what you are affirming is possible.

7. Accentuate the positive in your affirmations. Never use negative affirmations.

8. After writing your affirmations, take action. Convert your dreams to reality.

Affirmations of Wealth

It will not be enough to simply read this book and the affirmations one time. Remember, repetition is vital to your success. Since many of the concepts introduced in this book will be new to you, it is recommended that you read with concentrated effort. Make sure you have a good grasp of the concept presented in each affirmation before reading the next one. Think about every affirmation and write your *Thoughts* and *Actions* in the appropriate sections after reading each affirmation. You will notice that your notes will create an interesting insight into your thoughts, desires and true beliefs. Your notes will come in handy when you write your own affirmations. Read each affirmation and the accompanying narration as many times as you must to "feel" its full impact. Use your "feelings," your emotions, as the basis of your self-discovery and as the foundation of your affirmations.

AFFIRMATIONS

FFIRMATION:

I AFFIRM MY BELIEFS EVERY DAY. I am able to maintain a healthy confidence in myself, in my God and in my ability to convert my dreams to reality, by affirming my faith, beliefs, desires and convictions every day.

𝒩ARRATION:

Confidence and belief in oneself are unquestionably vital to achieving any goal or to fulfilling any mission in life. Daily affirmation of your beliefs, desires, convictions and faith is the most powerful tool known to develop self-confidence and to prepare your subconscious mind to convert your latent desires to action. Affirmations are most effective when they are self-written and invoke the powers of emotion. Also, affirmations are a confirmation of your inherent desires and, in some cases, your true destiny in life. When I affirm my beliefs, I continue to reaffirm my faith *in* myself, my abilities, my desire to succeed and my passion for fulfilling my God-given mission and purpose in life. What I *am, I affirm, and what I affirm, Iam.*

$\mathcal{W}$ISDOM FOR TODAY:

I will develop at least one significant affirmation. I will read this affirmation every day with belief and conviction. I will add one affirmation to my affirmation journal each day until I have revealed all of my true desires and aspirations. I will convert these desires and aspirations to reality by applying and affirming my faith.

$\mathcal{T}$HOUGHTS: _____

_____
_____
_____
_____
_____
_____
_____
_____

$\mathcal{A}$CTIONS: _____

_____
_____
_____
_____
_____
_____
_____

FFIRMATION:

I HAVE RELEASED MY ATTACHMENT TO THE PAST.

I forgive others and myself for past experiences. I know this forgiveness will free my energy to create positive results.

*N*ARRATION:

Is there someone, or more than one person in your life, who you need to forgive? Forgiveness is one of the most powerful gifts that anyone can give because it benefits both the giver and the receiver. The act of forgiveness benefits the giver because it is an act of courage. Forgiving others relieves you of the negative emotions and burdens you have been carrying. The benefit to the receiver is also great. People who need forgiveness are seeking your kindness, love and leadership. They instinctively tear themselves down until you give them your forgiveness. If you truly want to fulfill any mission in life, if you truly want to create total wealth, you must release your burdens and those of others in your life. In forgiving, you must include forgiveness of yourself as well. What is past is gone. Learn from the past and move on. If you cannot achieve this state of mind, you cannot achieve true wealth because you will not be ready for it.

WISDOM FOR TODAY:

I will take action on my dreams, desires opportunities and obstacles today. If I wait until tomorrow, I dramatically reduce my chances for success and ultimately may not fulfill my own destiny.

THOUGHTS: _____

_____

_____

_____

_____

_____

_____

_____

ACTIONS: _____

_____

_____

_____

_____

_____

_____

I Am Fearless ™

AFFIRMATION:

I DEVELOP COOPERATIVE ALLIANCES WITH OTHERS.

I am sure that "no man is an island." I can only succeed when I develop and employ the talents of others through alliances of cooperative effort.

NARRATION:

How do great leaders truly succeed? Whether it is in business, family, politics, community activities or philanthropic endeavors, all great leaders employ the talents of others and create synergistic power in their organizations through strategic and cooperative alliances. For example, when I practiced law full time, I could not be successful unless my partner, our staff and I all cooperated and worked together in the creation and achievement of both personal and business goals. We had the same mission: to exceed our clients' expectations every day while maintaining the integrity of our firm. I could not accomplish this mission alone. It took the cooperation of all our employees, our vendors, our banks and our customers. I clearly explained our mission to all these different people and asked for their help. I defined the benefit to each of them and the benefit to me. With their help, loyalty, suggestions and cooperation, we created win-win situations for all involved. Since everyone clearly saw the benefit to our alliance and how we could all win, we all won. This same powerful strategy has been employed on a much larger scale by Henry Ford, Gandhi, Lincoln, the Founding Fathers of The United States and other great leaders. This is not an autocratic approach. Eventually all autocrats fail somehow, some way. Alliances of cooperative effort, people working together for the same cause and with the same values, create wealth for all those involved.

*W*ISDOM FOR TODAY:

I will seek out true relationships of cooperative effort, relationships where all parties win. When doing so, I make sure my value system is not compromised, and I form alliances with others whose integrity and ethics are above reproach.

*T*HOUGHTS: _____

_____

_____

_____

_____

_____

_____

_____

*A*CTIONS: _____

_____

_____

_____

_____

_____

_____

I Am Fearless™

FFIRMATION:

I LAUGH OFTEN. I refresh my soul every day with laughter.
Laughter has a healing effect on my mind and my body. It is good to
laugh heartily every day. I bring cheer to myself and to others when I
do so.

$\mathcal{N}$ARRATION:

Who said the world has to be a serious place all the time?
I can think of several people right now who I have not seen
laugh in months, maybe not in years. Laughter truly is
therapy for the mind and the soul. If I cannot find things to
laugh at or people to laugh with, I laugh at myself. I look
back at the laughable things I have done, or the good times
that I have enjoyed and I laugh. When I laugh, I relieve
stress, I create a positive frame of mind and I calm my soul. I
also laugh when faced with adversity. My faith and belief in
myself and in my mission is so strong that I know I am going
to overcome any obstacle, and I laugh at my past worries.

WISDOM FOR TODAY:

I plan to achieve my goals and realize my dreams, but I will also laugh along the way. I appreciate my accomplishments and I celebrate with good cheer. When I do so, I nourish my mind and my soul.

THOUGHTS: _____

_____

_____

_____

_____

_____

_____

_____

ACTIONS: _____

_____

_____

_____

_____

_____

_____

$\mathcal{A}$FFIRMATION:

I MAKE CLEAR AND DEFINITE DECISIONS. I realize that those who have a clear and definite purpose in life make clear and definite decisions. This is a characteristic of leadership. I make clear decisions after separating fact from fiction, then I pursue my findings with clarity of mind.

$\mathcal{N}$ARRATION:

Do you know anyone who can't make a decision or who labors over every decision they make? I would tend to bet this person is a follower (a person who instinctively follows others), not a leader. When you have a clear and definite mission and purpose in life and your vision is focused, it becomes very easy to make clear decisions. The inability to make a decision is generally based, like so many other insecurities, on fear. It could be fear of failure, fear of embarrassment or fear of being wrong. When you are truly fearless, and combine your fearlessness with definiteness of purpose, your ability to make good decisions, and thereby lead others, becomes readily apparent. When I refer to clear decisions, I also refer to decisions that are based on fact, not assumptions. In the business world, and in many other parts of our lives, when we assume, we are wrong. Followers assume things because they do not have the confidence to find out the true facts. Leaders have no fear of the truth and always want to know the true facts. Clear decisions based on fact, not emotions or hearsay, almost always lead to better solutions, better relationships and a better way of life.

WISDOM FOR TODAY:

I have the strength of character to find the true facts before making a decision. When I do so, I am clear and concise in my decisions. I lead, I do not follow.

THOUGHTS: _____

_____
_____
_____
_____
_____
_____
_____
_____

ACTIONS: _____

_____
_____
_____
_____
_____

I Am Fearless ™

AFFIRMATION:

I LISTEN TO THE WISDOM OF MY BODY. When my body sends me a message, I listen to it. I do not ignore the wisdom of my mind or body. Messages of comfort and discomfort are delivered to me for a specific reason. When I discover the reason for these messages, I immediately begin to heal myself.

NARRATION:

How many times have you failed to listen to your intuition and later regretted it? Well, the same theory holds true for the messages sent to you by your body. If you are tired, why don't you sleep? If you are in pain, why don't you stop what is causing the pain? The answers to these questions is usually, "I don't have enough time," or "I have more important things to do." Remember, you have been given a great gift by God. God has given you the ability to choose what you want to do. But stop and think for a moment. Do you make choices based on honest reflection and listening to your own wisdom, or do you make choices on impulse based on prior conditioning? If your answer is the latter, you may be in for some serious physical and emotional problems. Listen to your body. It always tells you what it needs. When you are thirsty it tells you to drink. When you are full, it tells you to stop eating. When you are tired, it tells you to sleep. When you are in pain, it tells you to stop. One of the oldest and most destructive mind-sets (one in which I used to strongly believe) is "no pain, no gain." But I have changed my mind-set to "no pain, utmost gain." In the long run, moderation is the key to any successful exercise routine. Listening to your body and the wisdom of nature within you is the door to true and total health.

WISDOM FOR TODAY:

Today I will allow my body to set its own limits. I will enjoy health through moderate exercise and a moderate diet. I will give my body and mind what they need, and I will have the self-discipline to control my excesses.

THOUGHTS: _____

_____

_____

_____

_____

_____

_____

_____

_____

ACTIONS: _____

_____

_____

_____

_____

_____

_____

I Am Fearless ™

AFFIRMATION:

I ENLIVEN MY IMAGINATION. Within my imagination lies all that I need to create wealth and to fulfill my God-given destiny. I inspirit my imagination with meditation, mindful awareness and spiritual music.

NARRATION:

There is incredible power stored within each of our minds, in our imaginations. The problem is that most people are so caught up in "doing," instead of "thinking," that they never use their imagination. I believe it was Dr. Albert Schweitzer who was once asked, "Doctor, what is the problem with our society today?" He responded, "Men simply don't think." Developing mental alertness is very similar to developing physical strength or physical endurance: you have to exercise your mind in order to develop it. How do you exercise your mind? You do it by reading, listening to tapes, meditating, writing, dreaming, reflecting and by learning from other great thinkers. When is the last time you read a short story or an essay by one of the great thinkers? When is the last time you solved a problem by thinking, rather than doing? Your mind already has the answers stored within it to solve almost every problem you could ever encounter. It has stored within it a creative power and an imagination that can make you wealthy, healthy and wise. It is your obligation to yourself, to your God and to society to eliminate whatever is preventing you from utilizing the full power of your creative imagination and to THINK.

𝒲ISDOM FOR TODAY:

I will exercise my thinking abilities today. I will not do anything mindlessly today. I will be aware of my thoughts, actions and words and I will THINK before I act.

𝒯HOUGHTS: _____

_____
_____
_____
_____
_____
_____
_____
_____

𝒜CTIONS: _____

_____
_____
_____
_____
_____

Your Spiritual Gold Mind

The Divine Guide to Financial Freedom

V. John Alexandrov

$\mathcal{I}$NTRODUCTION

Since publishing *Affirmations Of Wealth-101 Secrets Of Daily Success*, I've had the opportunity to travel throughout the country giving seminars and keynote speeches, as well as speak with thousands of people individually, about their personal challenges and successes in life. This has been, and continues to be, my mission and purpose in life—helping others to succeed and fully utilize their God given talents.

The more I listened to the common challenges we each face, the more I realized there is a common thread, a missing link, between professing our desire to be wealthy or successful, and actually attaining it. In other words, most people truly want to succeed and are willing to dedicate themselves to being and doing so, yet there is a dark mental cloud that continually drifts over us, preventing the rays of success from manifesting in our lives. So many people have told me, "they wish their prayers would be answered," or "they are doing all the right things," yet success seems as elusive as a mirage in the middle of the desert. I finally, after months of contemplating this issue, developed a new paradigm, a new way of looking at this challenge, the result of which is embodied in this book, Your Spiritual Gold Mind. After countless interviews and personal coaching sessions, I was enlightened to the following truths:

1. Most people want to succeed, they just don't know how to accept success. 2. Most people never become wealthy because they lack a truthful understanding of the relationship between God, themselves and money. 3. Most people associate success with money yet have

a poor relationship with money and what it actually represents. 4. All of us have a money heritage which either enhances or limits our ability to create, generate or accept wealth. 5. Having wealth and money (and maintaining and proliferating each one) is directly related to our inner spiritual economy.

6. Anyone can become successful and wealthy, spiritually and financially, after acknowledging and accepting the goodness of money. We can regenerate our ability to create wealth by following certain spiritual and money principles. 7. We each have a spiritual and financial gold mind within, which continually delivers to us exactly what we profess spiritually, verbally, mentally and physically. Our spiritual and financial gold mind mirrors our faith. 8. Our spiritual gold mind is waiting for each of us to tap into it for God's sake and for ours. 9. There is a manifestation process (a proven method) to claim, attain and accept wealth, spiritually and financially, that always works if we choose to have faith.

I must declare up front that this is not a "religious" book or a "religious" philosophy, nor does it contain a "religious" agenda. Your Spiritual Gold Mind is a book about intentioned enlightenment and the manifestation and acceptance of wealth, including money, through spiritual means. Nor is this book a "contemporary" thesis by a "contemporary" thinker about the development of prosperity. This is purely and simply a book which reveals the truth about wealth, and the spiritual and financial laws about wealth, money and prosperity, which have been utilized by millions of people for thousands of years. There have been so many "new age" prospectives bantered about in recent years that one begins to wonder, "what is the truth?" We read and hear things such as, "there is no right or wrong, only bi-polar experiences," or " our souls are experiencing what they must experience right now because in past lives we didn't experience these things." There are hundreds more new age doctrines such as, "we must disassociate ourselves from money and material things in order to find true prosperity." I have finally concluded, after interviewing thousands of people, that most of these new age doctrines are convenient excuses not to accept responsibility for our own personal choices.

Your Spiritual Gold Mind explains the truth about spiritual principles, the power of God, and the manifestation of all the good that is ours by birthright.

Please keep an important fact in mind while reading this book: there is power in simplicity. The principles you will be reading and implementing have been used for thousands of years. They were used by Moses, Jesus, Mother Teresa, as well as many of the great entrepreneurs of the world. They are used daily to manifest dreams and goals of all types, and to glorify God for His love and greatness. These principles are used to create wealth of all types, and yes, to develop financial fortunes and material things. Contrary to the theories you may have read or heard elsewhere, in this book you will learn money is good; in fact, money is God in action. You will learn not to disassociate yourself from the real world, but how to use your divines to embrace and accept the abundance of the real world; as well as how to use it for the good of God, yourself and many other people.

We live in an ever changing world which tries to persuade

us to forget about principles and focus on new prospectives. I will admit, learning and implementing new prospectives can be invigorating and financially profitable. However, forgetting about spiritual principles, and how they apply to our individual and collective lives, is a sure path to destruction (history has proven this many times).

As you are reading this book, you may find some similarities to other practitioners of the gold mind principles: Jesus, many of the prophets, Florence Scovel Shinn, Dr. Joseph Murphy, Eric Butterworth, Shakti Gawain, Frederic Lehrman and John Randolph Price to name a few. I highly recommend you study their lives, read their works, and implement their doctrines as well, but try to do so in a modern day context. **Your Spiritual Gold Mind** takes the principles of love, prosperity, abundance, gratitude, truth, vision, faith, the spoken word, choice acceptance, wealth (and several others) and relates them to the realities of today's world. In the past, taxes, credit cards, electronic banking, e-commerce, and the Internet were not discussed in spiritual terms, nor were they taken into consideration when explaining the development and acceptance of money and financial wealth through spiritual principles. Today, however, all these things are a reality of life which we must understand in real and spiritual terms in order to establish and accept spiritual and financial freedom.

As you read this book, you will see scripture references at the conclusion of each affirmation. These have been included for those of you who enjoy, and include, Bible study as part of your daily life. I am not a theologian, nor do I have any theological training. The scripture references were collected be me during years of reading and study. At first glance, many of them may not seem to have a direct relationship to the affirmation you are reading; but if you do some research, you will find they are all related to this philosophy. Since the references were collected over a long period of time, you will see they have come from different Bible versions and may not exactly correspond to your Bible. For those of you who do not study or use the Bible, these scripture references are not necessary or crucial to the understanding and use of this book or the manifestation process. You may simply read them or not, but it will not diminish your understanding or the usefulness of this book if you do not read them.

It is my goal to help the countless people who are always striving and searching for success and wealth, to achieve (or maybe more importantly, to accept) them, whatever they represent for you. When you are reading and using **Your Spiritual Gold Mind**, please keep in mind the following:

1. Developing and accepting financial wealth is not a secret, it is a process.
2. We typically get from life what we prepare for, spiritually and financially.
3. We are all perfect expression's of God's love.
4. We live in a world of divine grace(a world of perfect abundance), not in a karmic world of give and take (limited abundance).

We all have been given almost unbelievable power from God; the ability to be love, give love, and receive love. We have been given the ability to dream, to act, and most importantly, to choose and accept (we can tap into the world of divine grace any time we want to). When we accept the truth about ourselves, accept the grace of God, and act in accordance with the divine plan of our lives, we can be, do and have all things. When we accept God, we can accept anything. When we work with God, we can work for anything. When we have God, we have everything.

How To Use This Book

The format of **Your Spiritual Gold Mind** is probably unlike any other book you have read or used. If you read Affirmations Of Wealth – 101 Secrets Of Daily Success, you are somewhat familiar with the process of reading with intention, self-discovery and journal writing. In Your Spiritual Gold Mind, the process of manifesting dreams and goals has been elevated to a new level. You will journey through a self-discovery process, read new insights (and discover new insights) about God, yourself and money, and you will put your thoughts into action through various spiritual and financial exercises.

I recommend you read through the entire book once before taking notes or completing the exercises. After you have read through the entire book, turn to the Spiritual And Financial Self-Discovery Checklist and complete the exercises that are appropriate for you. Then begin reading through the affirmations again. Some of them will "click" or "strike at your heart or soul." Take note of these affirmations and complete any recommended exercises. Also, after reading each affirmation, take notes in the "Thoughts" section reserved after each affirmation. Then write some short goals or priorities to complete in the "Actions" section. This will create a wonderful journal, treasure map and foundation for the realization of your dreams and goals.

There is no right or wrong way to use this book. Some

people read one affirmation a day, some more. Some people use specific affirmations as a guide to develop their own affirmations: this is great. I recommend you do the same as well. Read, and more importantly, USE this book. Do so at your own pace, in your own way. Personalize your book as much as possible. Write in it often and pay special attention to the notes. Most importantly, however, you must put your thoughts and what you learn into action. Have fun. Share your new insights with others. Create and share your wealth for God's sake and for yours.

The Meaning Of Words

Throughout this book, you will see several familiar terms which may have different meanings in the context of this writing than in every day use. Keep in mind when reading and using the principles in **Your Spiritual Gold Mind**, the power of the spoken and written word is extraordinary. The definitions of the following terms, and your use and understanding of them, will help you focus in, and fully utilize, the power of your gold mind.

God: As mentioned in the introduction to this book, this is not a "religious" philosophy; it is a spiritual philosophy. I have no desire to evoke a certain religion or religious philosophy as part of this process. We all have a spirituality about us, a spirit within us. There is no denying there is a God, a Creator or Infinite Intelligence in this universe that is far superior to us. We were created by God to live, prosper and proliferate abundance and His goodness every day. My personal belief is that God is the Holy Trinity, represented by the Father, Son and the Holy Spirit. I refer to God as "He" and "Him" because my Savior, Jesus Christ, continually refers to God as "My Father." Your beliefs may be different. *The basic nature of this book and the fundamental spiritual and financial principles herein are temporal; they apply to people of all religions, all faiths and to anyone who is secular in thinking as well.* If you want or need to substitute the word God with the words "Higher Power" or "Creator" or something similar, do so. But make sure you stay true to the processes revealed in this book.

Wealth: Fundamental to the understanding of this philosophy is that wealth and money are very separate and distinct things. Wealth is much more than money, cars or lavish homes. There are many people who obtain many material possessions but never become wealthy because they lack a basic understanding of truth, spirituality and personal responsibility in their lives. Wealth is a balance of spiritual fulfillment and devotion as well as love, physical and mental health, family happiness, true friendships, social kindness—as well as money. Now don't deceive yourself into financial poverty or mediocrity because you think money isn't important.

Money is as important as all other forms of wealth. It is my goal to help you create, attract and circulate all types of wealth in your life, including money.

Prosperity: Many people confuse the words "prosperity" and "abundance." You will see me use both words several times in this book, many times in the same affirmation. Prosperity means success or financial well being. The term prosperity carries with it a feeling of progressiveness. Prosperity relates financial and personal success with action; developing and maintaining a thriving life spiritually, physically and financially. But in its most basic form, prosperity means financial or economic success.

Abundance: To be abundant, or to have abundance, means to have plenty, have more than enough, or to be bountiful. This is not an economic or financial term, although we can enjoy financial abundance. Abundance is a natural state of being; it requires no effort, only an understanding, consciousness and dedication to living in an abundant state of mind. Remember that our physical realities are a true reflection of our inner realities. Living an abundant life spiritually and mentally leads to an abundant life physically and financially.

Riches: Again, although many people perceive the term "rich" to be a financial state, the truest definition of the word rich means to be fruitful or fertile. In other words, people who are rich are full of ideas and actions which, when cultivated, produce remarkable returns. These returns may be spiritual, financial or both. People who   are rich continuously harvest and replenish themselves and others with love, spirit, thoughts, actions and money.

Money: Money, in a very real sense, is something accepted or given as a medium of exchange. Money can be represented by many things, but for most people it is represented by cash (dollar bills, coins, etc.). Money can also be abstract. For example, promissory notes, certificates of deposit and stock certificates represent money, but not in the form of cash. As we earn or attract more money, we typically convert it from the real form (cash), into money in the abstract (certificates of deposit, etc.). Money, as described in this book, is also a form of energy with incredible properties, just like many other forms of energy. We pass on our individual energy (our thoughts, dreams, love, hate, envy, etc.) when we use or invest our money. Our money is the physical representation of our thoughts and beliefs which carries forth a part of us everywhere it goes.

Manifestation: The term manifestation means to develop into physical reality. I continually use the words manifest and manifestation in this book and the related exercises. You will read about (and hopefully use) a "manifestation process" which will help you convert your spiritual and mental energy into physical reality. So manifestation is a process of converting thoughts into physical reality.

Faith: An entire book could be written about this one word. As described here, the term faith means belief coupled with action; the ability to take action on your dreams and goals and to follow the divine plan of your life, even though you may not see any physical evidence of their manifestation. Faith also describes your commitment to God's plan for your life, trusting that this is the right plan for you (and for Him), and carrying out your divine plan to completeness. Remember that faith without action is dead (it is no faith at all). Belief and trust in God, and the unseen, while maintaining your faith as evidenced by your actions; this is true faith.

Spiritual/Spirituality: You will see the term spiritual throughout the upcoming pages. For a word that seems so obvious, it is very difficult to describe what spirituality really is. I think the best way to describe someone who is spiritual is to characterize them as godlike. Spiritual people have many godlike attributes. They are blessed in thought and action, boundless in their love, virtuous and pure in their intentions, yet they are all powerful. You will see me refer to the "spiritual economy" several times. And the very title of this book, Your Spiritual Gold Mind, portrays our ability to live abundant, prosperous and faithful lives through spiritual thoughts and actions (by becoming one with God in conscious intention and through our actions). Look again at the key words in the definition of the word spiritual; godlike, blessed, divine, boundless, virtuous, all powerful, pure, eternal, devout. These words not only depict the concept of spirituality, they set forth our goal; to be spiritual in all that we are and all that we do. This is true spirituality. Truth: When we are truthful with ourselves, we exhibit and confirm our integrity, genuineness, authenticity and fidelity. Truth is a principle, similar to love; it is eternal, unlimited in scope and application, as well as necessary for spiritual awakening and development. Think about these examples for a moment:

1. When we are true to God and His divine plan for our lives, we confirm our very reason for being. We are authentic, honest and humble.

2. When we are true to ourselves, we are genuine in thought and action and we exhibit fidelity to our very being through faith.

3. When we are true to our calling, we confirm our belief and faith in God and to our personal integrity.

4. When we do all things with truth, we develop freedom through spirituality and principle centered living. There is a quote inscribed on the face of the courthouse in my hometown. It reads " Obedience To Law Is Liberty." The same holds true for our dedication to living a spiritual and truthful life; when we are obedient and surrender to God, His plan, His love, and truly think and act spiritually, we are liberated.

Investment: When we "invest" something or "invest in" something, we are taking an empowering action. You will soon learn, when we invest in something our mentality and the very essence of who we are travels with our investment. We actually infuse ourselves into the company, person or relationship we invest in. Be very careful when investing love, time and energy (including your money), because your results typically will reflect your mentality at the time you invest. Always be spiritual in your thinking and in your actions when investing anything—then you will see marvelous returns.

Grace: We live in a world of grace; a world of love, thanksgiving, beauty and perfect abundance. This is the natural world God created and established for us; not a world of give and take, lack or limitation. The only lack or limitation we ever experience is created by us, through our thoughts, actions (or inaction) and lack of faith. Perfect abundance is all around us and in us; it is right before our eyes. All we have to do is attune ourselves to it by loving God, devoting to His plan for our lives, and accepting the flow of wealth that is ours by birthright. Grace and abundance are the natural way.

Divine/Divines: I have already referred to the "divine plan" several times in this book and you will see it many more times. We each have a purpose, as well as many unique God given talents. Our divine self is the self God intended us to be. We each have godlike qualities and an all-knowing intuition. We each have a truth that was established just for us. When we find our truth (or surrender to it), use our godlike qualities, and do so to carry out God's intended purpose for us, we are divine.

Success: One of the greatest definitions of success I have ever seen/heard was described by Napoleon Hill as, "having anything you want in life without violating the laws of God or the rights of other people." I would alter this slightly and describe success *as being, manifesting, having or accepting anything you want in life without violating the laws of God, without violating your individual truth (devoting yourself to God's divine plan for you), and without violating the rights of other people.*

Financial Freedom: Financial freedom is a state of consciousness in which you can be, do or have anything—regardless of the amount of money you have.

The Spiritual Economy

The spiritual economy is a state of consciousness. In the truest sense, spiritual economies are created when we discover, attune ourselves with, and surrender to God's divine plan for our lives. When this happens, we become a consciousness with and for God and we open the channels for amazing flows of abundance and prosperity. Our individual spiritual economies thrive and regenerate on love, gratitude, faith, acceptance, divine devotion and truth. It seems strange doesn't it; describing the economy in terms of truth and love instead of gross national product or interest rates? But the key to our individual prosperity and to the collective long term wealth of any nation, is consciousness. As we individually and collectively move closer to, and establish ourselves in the consciousness of God, we prosper in all aspects of our lives. Lasting financial wealth requires a spiritual commitment, spiritual investments and spiritual accountability; the willingness to give and receive love, wealth and God's direction and goodness in every aspect of our lives.

As a result of creating and proliferating our individual spiritual economies, we learn not only how to create a life of spiritual well being, but also how to open the channels for the manifestation of material wealth and money. Keep in mind, continuously, that money is good-money is God in action. However, our focus must always be on God first, and the good we can create for Him as a result of our dedication to His plan, with His love. *If we begin to idolize money or material things, we shall have sinned and we shall be broke. The manifestation of money must come as a result of who we are, and the love, time and energy we give or invest in the truth.*

Therefore, it should be our goal to glorify God in our thoughts and actions; to become one with the Divine Mind, the consciousness of God. Our spirit, our very thoughts and our very soul always travel with our energy, including our money. To create and manifest wealth, we must give wealth. To create and manifest love, we must give love. To create and manifest abundance, we must be abundant. This is the only true way to manifest wealth and continuously replenish the universe and ourselves with prosperity.

Our Money Heritage

For many of you, this is the moment you have been waiting for; now we are going to start talking about money. Just as we each have a genetic heritage, we each have a money heritage as well. With near certainty, we take on the characteristics of our family's money genealogy. Think back to the way your parents or other close family members handled their financial affairs, then take a good hard look at your financial situation right now. How many similarities are there? It is astonishing, isn't it? Think about the spending, savings and debt patterns of your parents. Are yours similar? More importantly, think back to some initial impressions or thoughts your parents instilled in you about money or financial affairs. What were they, and how have they affected your life? If you are really honest, you will agree they have had a dramatic impact on your life.

As you read the *Affirmations For Spiritual And Financial Enrichment*, you will notice several affirmations on this subject. Why? Because what we consciously and unconsciously learned and absorbed from our parents has a tendency to stay with us forever. If your parents tended to "play it safe," you will have a strong tendency to do the same. If your parents were "gamblers," always taking risks, you most likely will do so as well. If your parents were always in debt, buying things on credit, or felt guilty about money, that may also be your perceived fate. If your parents were responsible with their money, invested it wisely and manifested wealth truthfully, most likely you will as well. Atypical pattern I often see is people striving and working hard to be successful, but financial emergencies and losses continue to manifest in their lives. This is primarily due to a deep seeded family heritage of lack, limitation, guilt, jealousy or emotional deceit. We each have a defining moment, or series of defining moments, in our financial lives. These defining moments typically occurred when we were young. We may have lost some money and were chastised for it publicly. We may have been told that people with money are "bad." We may have been told we must work hard for our money, resulting in a "work hard" heritage instead of a "creating wealth and prosperity" heritage. I could go on and on, but a crucial exercise for you to do right now is to take out a pen and a piece of paper, and write down the most vivid experiences you had with money as a child. What do you remember about money? Why do you remember this? Were your first money experiences pleasurable or painful? Why? When you manifest wealth and receive money, do you feel guilty or ashamed about it? Why? Do you have a hard time accepting money or gifts? Why? If you become successful, do you feel as if you will betray your family heritage? Why? Continue on and write down all your feelings about money, what your current financial situation is, and why you believe you created the financial condition (good or bad) you are in right now. This may be a painful exercise for you, but doing so will bring into your consciousness all of your feelings, emotions, fears and beliefs about money. *And remember, consciousness is one of the keys to financial freedom.*

Self-Worth vs. Net Worth

Our self-worth should never be determined by our net worth. Take a look at the definition of financial freedom again: financial freedom is a state of consciousness in which you can be, do or have anything regardless of the amount of money you have. In other words, you can remain true to yourself and your calling regardless of whether you have a few dollars or millions of dollars. We are directed, and we are obligated to each live a rich and fulfilling life whether we have money or not. *A few words of caution here. This book is going to help you manifest anything you want in life, including money, but do not allow the size of your bank account to determine the quality of your life. Be true to God's principles, continually enrich yourself and others, and you will be wealthy-personally and financially.*

Our self-worth should never be determined by our net worth, but our net worth may be, and most often is, determined by our self-worth. In other words, in order to be financially wealthy, you must believe you are worthy of it. The main reason most people do not achieve financial wealth and freedom is because of fear, low self-esteem, a poor money heritage and/or emotional heritage, or because they have an addiction (addictions are many times the result of your emotional heritage, fear or low self-esteem). Let's take a look at each of these challenges to personal and financial freedom to see how they affect our financial lives and our personal spiritual economy.

Fear

The only two natural fears we have are the fear of falling and the fear of loud noises. Where did the rest come from? We inherit fears through watching and listening to other people, by watching television, and from absorbing other unwarranted and fearful information. If we are a fearful person, we are most likely fearful financially as well. Many people have specific money fears which inhibit them their entire lives, and which create a fearful money heritage for generations. What are your fears about money? How did these develop in your life? Why do you have these fears?

Keep in mind an important fact; money is innocent. Money cannot perpetuate fears, solve problems or create wealth. Only people can do these things. If you are a fearful person and you create more financial wealth, you will be more fearful with (an maybe of) your money. If you are a fearless person, you will continue to be fearless with your money. So, an important step in developing financial freedom is eliminating (or at least properly managing) fear. If you live in fear, no matter how much money you have, you can never be financially free. In the Affirmations For Spiritual And Financial Enrichment, there are several affirmations that will help you with this. Use these affirmations often. They will help you to clear the channel for the manifestation of your desires.

Erasing The Old Myths About Money

There are several myths about money which must be addressed, understood and eliminated before manifesting financial wealth. The first is the age old lie... money is the root of all evil. Many people live their entire lives innocently perpetuating this lie. They claim since this quote has a Biblical foundation and is embodied in scripture, this must be true. If you do your homework, you will find this reference is neither Biblical or anywhere in scripture. If you read the Gospel according to John, you will see he said, "The love of money is the root of all evil." In other words, we cannot idolize money. Idolatry is a sure path to self destruction. Money, by itself, cannot create evil or do evil things. Only people can create or do evil things. *Money is good, money is innocent, money is pure; it is only our intentions that can destroy the goodness of money.*

The next myth we often hear is that in the Book Of Revelation, Jesus said, "A camel would fit through the eye of a needle before a rich man would enter the kingdom of heaven." Go back and look at the definition of the term "rich." Rich is not a financial term, it is a description of a state of consciousness or a state of mind. Jesus was referring to people who are rich in conceit, selfishness and self-aggrandizement. He wasn't referring to people who were financially well-off. *In order to enter the kingdom of heaven, which by the way lies within you and is all around you, you must be rich in love, thought and action.*

Another myth which devastates many people is the concept that they must "suffer" or "sacrifice greatly" now in order to enter the Promised Land or in order to display religious piety. Discipline certainly is a key to spiritual and financial freedom, suffering is not. *The spiritual economy, living in a world of grace and perfect abundance, living as an expression of God's love, requires no sacrifice.* What they require is love, the glorification of God through prosperous and abundant thoughts and actions, and constant gratitude and replenishment. Forget about suffering and sacrifice and focus on how you are going to glorify God through your thoughts, action and love. The final myth we will address here (there are others addressed in the affirmations) is the myth that hard work leads to financial freedom. Quite honestly, I have seen hard work ruin many lives and devastate the money heritage of many families. If you are true to your calling, glorify God through your thoughts, actions and chosen profession... and you love what you do, how can this be hard work? Many people work so hard to "make a living," they have no room for abundance and prosperity. They are so focused on surviving, they have no time or energy to live. Many people use "hard work" as an excuse or justification for mediocrity or financial indifference. They say, "after all, I am working so hard, I don't have the time or energy to do what I really want to do." Although hard work certainly can be a noble attribute, it has almost no bearing on the manifestation of financial wealth. If you view what you do as hard work, you should seriously consider changing professions. *You must love what you do and do what you love; this is the path to spiritual and financial freedom.*

Eliminate these myths from your thinking. Replenish yourself, spiritually and financially, with thoughts of abundance, love and the glorification of God. From here you can manifest everything which is yours by divine right.

Contact Information

V. John Alexandrov
c/o Legacy Capital Solutions, LLC
10 Chestnut Street – Suite 640
Worcester, MA 01608

Websites

www.themoneychi.com
www.legacycapitalsolutions.com

Email

johna@themoneychi.com

General Questions

info@themoneychi.com

Media Partner – Website Administration

Asagio Media Interactive, Inc.
67 Millbrook Street – Suite 113
Worcester, MA 01606

www.asagiomedia.com

Ordering Information

You may order additional copies of this book
by visiting our website at www.themoneychi.com.

Bulk sale discounts are available.
Contact Mike Surabian at mike@themoneychi.com

To order hard copies of
Affirmations of Wealth and Your Spiritual Gold Mind
contact us at
info@themoneychi.com

Speaking Engagements

To inquire about hiring John to speak at your event,
contact him at johna@themoneychi.com.